The Female PROPHETS OF THE BIBLE

WHO WERE THEY, AND WHAT DID THEY HAVE TO SAY?

THE REV. DEBRA MOODY BASS, PH.D

WESTBOW
PRESS®
A DIVISION OF THOMAS NELSON
& ZONDERVAN

The Holy Bible: New Revised Standard Version. 1989. Nashville: Thomas Nelson Publishers.

WestBow Press books may be ordered through booksellers or by contacting:

WestBow Press
A Division of Thomas Nelson & Zondervan
1663 Liberty Drive
Bloomington, IN 47403
www.westbowpress.com
1 (866) 928-1240

ISBN: 978-1-9736-1183-7 (sc)
ISBN: 978-1-9736-1182-0 (e)

Print information available on the last page.

WestBow Press rev. date: 12/28/2017

Contents

Introduction

The second major section of the Old Testament (after the Torah) is the prophets. The Hebrew word *"navi"* and the Greek word *"propheteous"* is used throughout both the Old and New Testaments to describe persons - both male and female – who received messages from God. The prophets were told to deliver these messages to an audience. The size of the audience did not matter, however, the message was crucial to the survival and preservation of the whole community.

There are many books about the biblical prophets. Most of these books focus only on the male prophets. The purpose of this book is to place emphasis on those prophets who were female, their story, their message and their audience. The female prophets covered in this book are: Miriam, Deborah, Huldah, Anna, and the four daughters of Philip. Each of these women were called "prophets or prophetesses" by the final editors of the Bible.

Yet when one compares these 8 women to the 15 male prophets who have books named after them in the Bible, there is a definite difference in the prophetess' delivery of God's message to their designated audiences. These differences have often allowed these 8 women to remain invisible and absent in the category of "prophet." Instead, they have been lumped together as part of a list referred to as "Women in the Bible."

It is this author's intent to bring these 8 women back into the forefront of their called profession as "prophets" of God. Their message was relevant then and is very relevant today.In this study of the female prophets two questions are asked: "What is her story?" and "What is her message?" The methodology that will provide answers to these questions is 3-fold: 1) Literary concerns (*hymn, narrative, poetry, or exhortation*); 2) Historical concerns (*What was the Sitz im Leben – situation that brought the need for a prophetic word?*); and 3) Theological concerns (*What is the God-human meaning in the text?*). In summary, I will show that the title of "prophetess" was validated in the text and her message was relevant to Israel's identity as the chosen people of God and as a light to the nations.

Dedicated to my son, Joshua Daniel Bass
And my late Mom, Lillie Bell Douglas Moody

"Whoever welcomes a prophet as a prophet will receive a prophet's reward, and whoever welcomes a righteous person as a righteous person will receive a righteous person's reward."

—Jesus, Matthew 10:41

MIRIAM
WHO WAS SHE?

Daughter, Sister, Singer, Wife, Mother, Prophetess

MIRIAM: WHAT IS HER STORY
(Exodus 2:4; 15:20-21; Num 12; 20:1; Deut 24:9; Micah 6:4)

The story of Miriam is found in the Torah, also known as the first five books of Moses *(Genesis, Exodus, Leviticus, Numbers and Deuteronomy)*. The Torah is a compilation of writings by several sources. It is the foundation for understanding God's intervention in history and God's relationship with his chosen people the Jews. Scholars have tried to narrow down the sources through a theological tool known as the Documentary Hypothesis.

In the Documentary Hypothesis, four main writers are believed to have authored their different traditions and a later redactor brought them together in the order we have them today. The four main writers are: the Yahwist writer (J) believed to have written in the 10th century BCE; the Elohist writer (E), believed to have written in the 9th-8th centuries; the Priestly writer (P), writes during the Babylonian Exile of the 6th century BCE; and finally the Deuteronomist writer (D) believed to have written in the late 6th and early 5th centuries in response to why God allowed the Babylonians to destroy Jerusalem and take God's chosen people into exile.

We first hear about "Moses' sister," Miriam, in Exodus 2:4: *"His sister stood at a distance, to see what would happen to him."* What is her story? The children of Israel are still in the land of Egypt when a new Pharaoh comes to power. This Pharaoh is not particularly fond of the multitude of Hebrews residing within the borders of Egypt.

It is obvious from the text that the dreams of Joseph, that once saved Egypt from a great famine, were now forgotten. Some scholars argue that Egypt was under foreign control during the time of the great famine by a people known as the Hyksos, from the north, who may have also been Semites.[1] This would explain how a foreigner like Joseph, could rise to such a high level of power in the Egyptian government. Then at a later time, Egypt was able to regain control of her government and overthrow the foreign yoke.

If this is the case, then fear of new invasions were probably a concern of the Pharaoh and his administration. Once he realized how rapidly the Hebrews multiplied, the thought entered his mind that in the threat of an invading foreign power, whose side would these non-Egyptians take? So for this new Pharaoh it was a matter of homeland security.

After attempting to handle the situation secretly by telling the midwives to kill all male babies born failed, the Pharaoh took drastic measures and commanded that all males born to the Hebrew women be thrown into the Nile River. This is where the story of Miriam began. She is one of three female characters in God's plan to deliver the Hebrews from Egyptian oppression: Jochebed – Moses' mother, Miriam – Moses' sister, and the daughter of the Pharaoh, who draws Moses from the water and raises him in the Pharaoh's palace.

Moses' mother refused to allow her 3-month old baby boy, to suffer the fate of Pharaoh's command. When she saw that he was a fine and good child, she knew that God had something special planned for his life. So she took matters into her own hands, with the help of her daughter, Miriam.

Jochebed makes a basket and plastered it with bitumen and pitch so that it would float. She put Moses in the basket and set him assail among the reeds. Miriam followed the basket to determine where it would end up. It ended up in the wading pool of the Pharaoh's daughter. She had pity on the Hebrew child and took him in as her own. Miriam stepped forth out of the bulrushes to ask the daughter if she wanted a Hebrew mother to nurse the child. She agreed and Miriam brought Moses' biological mother to nurse him. So even as a young child, Miriam is looking out for others and her quick wit *(the wisdom of God?)* allows her brother Moses to be nursed by his biological mother. *(Exodus 2:7-8)*.

Miriam does not encounter her baby brother again until he is an adult

---

[1] Harris, Stephen L. *Understanding the Bible.* 8th edition, McGraw Hill: New York, 2011, p 94

and returns from a self-imposed exile in Midian. Moses fled from Egypt after he killed an Egyptian guard in self-defense. There he met and married his wife, Zipporah, a daughter of the priest of Midian. She bore him a son, Gershom. God now decides to use all three of Jochebed's children to deliver the Hebrews from Egyptian slavery: Miriam, Moses, and Aaron. Referred to as prophets by Micah (6:4), together they accept the leadership role God appoints them to, as prophets to His people in Egypt. Although it is obvious that Moses is the primary leader, Miriam and Aaron have comparable and necessary roles to help this hope of deliverance become a reality.

> *Then the prophet Miriam, Aaron's sister, Took a tambourine in her hand; And all the women went out after her with tambourines and with dancing.*
>
> *—Exodus 15:20*

This appears to be a rescue narrative.[2] The main characters are 3 unnamed women – Pharaoh's daughter, Moses' sister, and Moses' mother. The 3 women unintentionally work together for the preservation of a baby, not aware of the major role Moses will play in Israel's history.

Who is Miriam? She is the eldest daughter of Jochabed and Amram. She was the big sister to Moses and Aaron. Although usually her name is omitted (Exo 6:20), as was the case with so many biblical women, she is eventually identified and given a name - Miriam (Num 26:59; I Chron 6:3; Micah 6:4). It is in her role as a *"prophetess"* that she will be examined in this book.

Miriam's name has been interpreted to mean *"bitterness"* by Jewish rabbis and *"star of the sea"* by the great theologian and writer of the Vulgate (Latin translation of the Bible), Jerome.[3] Today's interpreters translate the word to mean *"plump one"* from the Hebrew root *"mra"*. Another translation is *"the wished for child"* from the Arabic *"mar-am."* Some scholars suggest it is

---

[2] Breuggemann, *Exodus: New Interpreter's Bible Commentary.* Vol 1, Abingdon Press: Nashville, 1998. pp 700-701.
[3] Ross, J. F. *Interpreter's Dictionary of the Bible.* New York: Abingdon Press, 1962, p 402.

originated from the Egyptian *"mer"* meaning *"love"*, or *"the beloved."*[4] The word for sister suggests it could mean *"to mend."*[5] The Septuagint (LXX) has *"Mariam,"* which is New Testament Greek for *"Mary."* It was a common name in New Testament times with its many variations.[6]

From the biblical texts, Miriam is an honored member of the community. She functioned alongside her priestly brother, Aaron in Numbers 12:1-2 and she is referenced to serving women in the Tent of Meeting .[7] She is the sister of a priest- Aaron. She is a musician and choral leader. All the women follow her lead when she breaks out into song. The women also follow her in prayer. Some scholars think there may have been other celebrative stories of Miriam, but they were suppressed after her conflict with Moses.[8]

Miriam stood up against her brother due to her weariness from years of wandering, and perhaps also because Moses remarried a Cushite woman of color (Num 12:1-15). Moses married outside the faith, and culture. But perhaps having been brought out of Egypt, he felt a more kindred spirit to a Cushite than a Hebrew. Although women did not rebuke men in public, Miriam felt empowered because of her status as a *"prophetess."* Miriam felt justified in questioning her brother's actions. She felt the need to be included in whatever plan God shared with Moses and Aaron. At one point she even questioned if God knew where they were going!

Miriam meant for her voice to be heard. She had given up family and home and just wanted to be heard and not invisible.[9] The conflict reflects a divided community. People were taking sides – Moses, Aaron, or Miriam. Marrying the Cushite woman brought the unrest among the people to a head.[10]

This challenge against Moses' leadership was a challenge against God.

---

[4] *Ibid*

[5] Siddons, Philip. *Speaking Out For Women – A Biblical View.* Valley Forge: Judson Press, 1980, p 54

[6] *Ibid*

[7] Reuther, Rosemary Radford, ed. *Religion and Sexism: Images of Woman in the Jewish and Christian Traditions.* New York: Simon and Schuster, 1974. P 68

[8] Williams, Michael E. ed. *The Storyteller's Companion to the Bible.* Vol 4, *Old Testament Women.* Nashville: Abingdon, 1993. p 69

[9] Kimbrough, Marjorie. *She Is Worthy: Encounters with biblical Women.* Nashville: Abingdon Press, 1994, p 26

[10] Williams, *The Storyteller's Companion…*p 74

In Numbers 12:6-9, God speaks to the trio making it clear that Moses is the spokesperson and if anyone speaks against him, there will be consequences. He was like no other prophet and beheld the face of God. It was upon God's departure that Miriam became leprous, a consequence of her speaking against Moses. Yet, because of her brother Moses' compassion and prayer life, God restored her to health after only 7 days outside the camp. Moses did not move forward until Miriam could return to the fellowship. The rabbis say God examined Miriam and declared her clean.[11]

Many feminists questioned why Miriam and not Aaron, was punished for challenging Moses' authority. Explanations range from the tradition that it was taboo for a woman to challenge a man, especially in public, to she was arrogant and her anger stemmed from her heart to the sin of Eve, wanting to know as much as God. Whatever the reason, Miriam's punishment served as an example to all not to question God's prominent spokesperson – Moses. Israel was a patriarchal society and women found their place in the role of family – daughter, sister, wife, or mother.[12]

There is no record of Miriam ever having married. This is unusual since the role of wife and mother were positions aspired to. These roles gave women validation and security in a hostile male environment. Tradition has it that she was married to a Caleb, one of the spies who came back with a positive report. They had a son named Hur. Hur was one of the men who held up Moses' arm when he was praying at the battle at Rephidim (Exod 17:10-12; 24:14). He was later murdered because he tried to stop the worshipers of the Golden Calf.[13]

Miriam embraced her role as a leader of all women. She led them in song and praise and prayer. She was the one who they could talk to when family and perhaps female health issues were of concern. Although tradition has Moses singing this song later, Miriam sings it differently because they had different leadership styles.[14]

Miriam's style was complimentary. This, according to Scanzoni and

---

[11] *Ibid.* p 76

[12] Kimbrough, Marjorie. *She Is Worthy...*, p 25

[13] Mindel, Nissan. *Miriam.* www.chabad.org/library/article_cdo/aid/112070/jewish/Aaron-and-Miriam.htm Kehot Publication Society

[14] *Ibid.* p 26

Hardesty, is one of four approaches to male/female relationships in the Bible. In their theory, "Each sex is considered equal in ultimate worth, but each has its own sphere to fill."[15]

Miriam's style was loud and enthusiastic, where Moses was more an introvert, reluctant to accept leadership without the prompting of God. Moses wanted everyone to be still and know God as he knew Him. Rosemary Radford Reuther says the following about Miriam's role in the book of Exodus:

> Even where a woman has attained legendary stature, the roles played by women in these writings are almost exclusively subordinate and/or supporting roles. Women are adjunct to men, characters necessary to a plot that revolves about males…These are necessary to the drama, and may even steal the spotlight occasionally but the story is rarely about them.[16]

Only Deborah, Jezebel, Miriam and Huldah stand on their own feet. But too little evidence survives about them to assess their actual position in Israel's society or their representiveness.[17]

As prophetess Miriam carries the torch for all women who have heard the calling of God on their lives, and accepted it, despite the obstacles and naysayers who refute and deny their anointing and right to speak on behalf of the Almighty God. Her name was Miriam – a wife, mother, prophetess, leader, singer, and teacher. She was a woman of self-esteem, a sister, a nationalist. She was equal to the task assigned to her hands because she was the daughter of a strong and defiant woman – Jochabed. Her mother was a courageous woman who defied the Pharaoh and preserved her son, Moses' life because she could see God in his face.

One story in the Midrash says Miriam studied the Law and defends her

---

[15] Scanzoni, Letha D. and Hardesty, Nancy A. *All Were Meant to Be*. Nashville: Abingdon Press, 1986, p 29. *The other 3 approaches are: debarment, synthesis, and transcendence.*

[16] Reuther, Rosemary Radford, *Images of Women in the Jewish and Christian Traditions*. P 60

[17] *Ibid.* p 61

mother and all the other women in a court of law when their husbands tried to do away with them. Therefore, she is considered the first woman lawyer.[18]

Miriam does not enter the Promised Land – nor do her brothers. They all died within 12 months of each other.[19] Moses led the people into the wilderness of Zin. The people stayed in Kadesh. Here is where Miriam died and was buried.[20] Some estimate her age at 126 years old.[21] She was the first of the 3 children of Jochabed and Amram to depart in the wilderness. The mention of her death is brief and not the main topic of the chapter - water was the concern of the people (Nu 20).

Yet her song was so influential that it lives on and continues to be sung by generations of women. As we move to the next chapter, we will discuss Miriam's message. This is found in the Song of Miriam. In this Song Miriam's words as a prophet of Israel, come through loud and clear.

---

[18] Siddons, Philip. *Speaking Out for Women – A Biblical View.* p 44
[19] Mindel, Nissan. *Miriam.*
[20] Numbers 20:1
[21] Mindel, Nissan. *Miriam.* www.chabad.org/library/Miriam.htm

MIRIAM'S MESSAGE OF PROPHECY

*"Then the prophet Miriam, Aaron's sister, took
a tambourine in her hand; and all the women
went out after her with tambourines and with
dancing. And Miriam sang to them:
'Sing to the Lord, for he has triumphed gloriously;
horse and rider he has thrown into the sea'"*

—Exod 15:20-21

The Song of Miriam follows the hymnic form: it praises the Lord in the first line and gives the reason for the praise in the second line. This hymn provides the opening couplet to the Song of Moses.

There were no collections preserved of the women prophets. Miriam's Song is one of the few exceptions to this rule. Walter Brueggeman argues that the older song is by Miriam and the women. It was later taken over by editors because Moses was the official leader.[22] According to Brueggeman, the women were the first witnesses but it took "the verification of the male leaders to authenticate their report."[23]

Miriam's message became the Song of Moses and the predominant message for generations of prophets/prophetesses to come. Miriam is finally named a prophetess (ha'navuja) in the Torah, not only in the Midrash. Her message is found throughout her life, but explicitly in Exodus 15:20. Miriam had experienced the whole gamut of what life had to offer: hope, despair, terror and deliverance, slavery and freedom, unimportance and prominence.[24]

Miriam played many roles that underlined her prophetic message to the women under her care. As a child and big sister, she was a protector of Moses. As a prophetess and co-leader, she was obedient, sensitive, mature, and for the most part, unselfish. In her final role as musician and songstress, she led the women to celebration and praise over the deliverance of God's people.

The words of the one verse are a repetition of the verses to the Song of Moses. Some scholars believe the Song was originally credited to Miriam, but the final editors chose to place Moses as the author.[25] The poem is often called the Song of Miriam. Usually poetic texts were independent in their existence before incorporated into the prose sections of the Hebrews scriptures.[26]

Miriam's first message to her audience is that God is a warrior. In this hymn "she interprets the actions of God to the people. God is a warrior.

---

[22] Brueggeman, Walter. *New Interpreter's Bible Commentary.* Vol I, p 799

[23] *Ibid*

[24] Kraft, Vicki. *Miriam,* https://bible.org//seriespage/lesson-1-miriam. July 12, 2007

[25] Williams, Michael E. *The Storyteller's Companion to the Bible,* p 68

[26] *Ibid*

He has defeated Pharaoh. God used the Sea as his weapon, God set up the Egyptians by making it look like Israel was trapped."[27]

God's actions against Egypt as displayed in the 10 plagues proved beyond a shadow of a doubt that God was a mighty warrior. The first singing (Moses or Miriam?) reiterates in detail the actions of God towards Egypt. These actions therefore, required and solicited the praise of the people. This praise is released in the form of singing and dancing. God is proclaimed as "my salvation" and "my strength and might."

Holy war does not require the strength or might of the people. It is all God's doing. God becomes our strength and might. As a warrior God, which was a familiar role of the gods of the Egyptians, this message encouraged and gave assurance of God's mighty protection against any and all enemies of the wandering Hebrew ex-slaves.

Miriam's second message to her audience is a message of unity. Although only one verse is recorded, it was probably the repetition of the earlier verses sung by Moses. "In that day they would sing in antiphonal singing – one side would sing and the other side would respond."[28] Here Miriam is called a "prophetess" (ha'navuj) for the first time. She situated the women in a circle (b'micholot). They held tambourines and began to dance within the circle.

The women did not separate themselves according to tribe or seniority. This new circle represented a new unity where each woman was equal and they had to work together if they and their families, would survive the unknown dangers of the wilderness wanderings.[29] Phillis Chester states that God's "Shechina is in the middle of this sacred circle. God's presence in the middle allowed each woman to feel close to God's presence."[30] The women felt God's presence in this unity circle the same way they felt God with them during childbirth. While in the sacred circle of unity, God allowed these women to see their past, present and future plights in the oneness of God.[31]

Miriam's third message as a prophetess is that God is a mighty deliverer.

---

[27] Ibid., p 69

[28] Ibid.

[29] Chester, Phillis. Miriam. The Phyllis Chester Organization. Jerusalem Post, April 18, 2014

[30] Ibid

[31] Ibid

In repetition of the Song of Moses, Miriam and the women declare God's deliverance in the future as it was on this day.[32] Israel will be delivered from the threat of any future enemies – Philistia, Edom, Moab, and Canaan. They will all fall in fear of what the God of Israel has done to Egypt on behalf of his chosen people Israel. No god in the past has been credited for such devastation towards forces that might hurt His own possession.

In Jeremiah 9:17 and 2 Chron 35:25 we learn that there were women skilled in dancing with joy and exultation when the military soldiers were victorious in battle. We see this especially on one occasion when David returned victorious over the enemies of Israel:

> As they were coming home, when David returned from killing the Philistine Goliath, the women came out of all the towns of Israel, singing and dancing, to meet King Saul with tambourines, with songs of joy, and with musical instruments. And the women sang to one another as they made merry; 'Saul has killed his 1000s and David his 10 thousands.'"
>
> —I Samuel 18:6-9

The presence of the professional singers was a sign to the people that victory over their enemies has occurred and the God who is responsible for such a victory should be praised and the people celebrate. This was a community at worship because its faith and hope and dependence on their God is more powerful as well as compelling than any situation they have encountered in the past and will encounter in the future.[33]

Miriam's voice was heard and the women followed her in prayer. The Hebrew women may have been the original audience of Miriam's message of unity, victory and Yahweh as a warrior God, but this same message was proclaimed by the prophets (both male and female) that followed her generation after generation.

This message remains as an underlying force embraced in the celebration

---

[32] Williams, Michael E. *The Storyteller's Companion to the Bible.* p 69
[33] *New Interpreter's Bible Commentary.* Vol 1, p 701

of Passover today. It is best said by the writer of this gospel song, *"Our God is an awesome God; He reigns from heaven above, in wisdom, power and love our God is an awesome God!"* Miriam was a prophetess. Her story predates the Deuteronomic Law which was used centuries later to suppress women in the New Testament period.[34]

---

[34] Mitchell, Ella Pearson. *To Preach or Not to Preach*, p 7

Chapter Two

DEBORAH
WHO WAS SHE?

Wife, Judge, Prophetess

DEBORAH: WHAT IS HER STORY?
(Judges 4-5)

The book of Judges is found in the Historical books of the Old Testament – Joshua-2 Kings. This is believed to be the work of the Deuteronomic Historian (DtH) in an attempt to justify Israel's demise and captivity. The DtH goes through Israel's past and highlights all of her sins against God thereby invoking the curses side of the covenant. The book of Judges in particular focused on the many times Israel sinned against God and God forgave her by sending a military leader (Judge) to deliver them from the hands of their enemies. However, after 13 references to Israel's apostasy, God had no choice but to allow Israel's enemies to defeat her.

The book of Judges contains the largest number of women characters of any book in the Bible – 19 in all. These stories told about women portray them as strong, heathy and faithful. The first 3 women are named, an unusual practice in the Bible. We find a wide spectrum of behaviors around women – both negative and positive in Judges.[35]

"At that time Deborah, a prophetess, wife of Lappidoth, was judging Israel" (Judges 4:4). Because there are so many women characters in the book of Judges, it then is no surprise that one of the judges in Israel was a woman. Her name was Deborah. Deborah's position of power during the times of the judges was one of the exceptions that even a patriarchal editor could not ignore, omit, or downplay.

Ella Pearson Mitchell says the following about Deborah:

---

[35] Olson, Dennis T. *The New Interpreter's Bible Commentary.* Vol 2, Nashville: Abingdon Press. 1998, p 782

The next woman to burst the bonds of the traditional limits on women was Deborah, well known as a military leader and ruling judge, but also a spiritual leader and "prophetess" (Judges 4:4). She was a popular counselor, the governor-judge, and the leader of the triumphant army. Rabbinical tradition has it that this "superwoman" rose from the lowly estate of lamp keeper in the tabernacle.[36]

The scriptures clearly refer to Deborah as a judge (military leader), a prophetess, and a wife. She was the only woman in all of scriptures who held that kind of leadership position and was blessed for it. Deborah was one of the few judges who actually achieved wisdom and settled cases while sitting under a palm tree of the same name, a palm of Deborah (Judges 4:5). It was as a practicing judge that God gave her a prophetic word to send to the army general – Barak, son of Abinoam – from Kadesh of the tribe of Naphtali.

Israelite women of the Bible found their identity first as a member of a family. Deborah was a daughter, a wife, a mother and a singer, like Miriam. Unlike some of the male prophets, choosing to be a full-time prophetess was not encouraged or even acceptable.[37]

Israel's agricultural based economy required both genders to work beyond the family household. Women worked in the fields gleaning (Ruth) and providing outside sources for their family's financial survival (the Virtuous Woman in Prov 31). It seemed to be the norm by the time of the Wisdom Literature that women had careers outside of the home.[38] This however, was unusual in the arena of politics and government. To be a female judge and prophetess is to reach a level of admiration and reverence that was very rare for women (at least as reported in the Bible).

Deborah's character must have been spectacular and unapproachable for her to be considered for this post. The text does not stipulate that only men

---

[36] Mitchell Ella Pearson. *To Preach or Not to Preach*, Valley Forge: Judson Press, 1991 *p 7-8*

[37] Scanzoni, *All Were Meant to Be*, p 57

[38] *Ibid.*, p 63-64

came to her seeking wisdom and advice, but says "and the Israelites came up to her for judgment." (Judg 5:4). This must have given her a high self-esteem.

In Miriam's case, she was pigeon-holed as a great leader of women, as if she could only prophesy in their presence. By the time of the Judges, this was not necessarily a limitation for Deborah. It appears from the text that Deborah was a well-known military leader (or advisor), a ruling judge, and a spiritual leader or prophetess.[39] Deborah was intelligent, wise, and gave advice that was received by all. When Deborah's advice projected future events, she became known as a prophetess because her wisdom and insight came from the Lord.[40]

Deborah's husband is Lappidoth. As tradition would have it, she is called Lappidoth's wife, even though she has accolades of her own. "The patriarchy of the day would not have allowed Lappidoth to be referred to as Deborah's husband."[41]

The book of Judges is a cyclical book that records Israel's cycle of sin-punishment-forgiveness-deliverance-sin again. It is reported at least 14 times. So once again, the previous judge (Ehud) died and Israel fell into sin again. This time the Lord sold them into the hands of King Jabin of Canaan, who reigned in Hazor. They were oppressed by King Jabin for twenty years. Then the people cried out to the Lord and the Lord spoke to Deborah a word of comfort and deliverance. She received it as a prophecy.

This prophecy was delivered to Barak, son of Abinoam from the town of Kadesh. Barak was a member of the Naphtali tribe of Israel. Yet, he knew that the Spirit of the Lord was upon Deborah, not so much him. Her reputation had preceded her.

Barak knew that with Deborah by his side, the scattered tribes would come together under his leadership and they would be victorious against King Jabin of Canaan. The twelve tribes were operating under a tribal confederacy. This was a loosely connected bond based on familial ties, not military obligation. So any tribe could refuse to come to another tribe's aide if they decided not to

---

[39] Mitchell, Ella P. *Women: To Preach or not to Preach...* p 7
[40] Kimbrough, Marjorie L. *She Is Worthy...* p 29
[41] *Ibid.*

fight on that day. The fact that Deborah's charisma was enough to unite the tribes under the battle cry, again says a great deal about her status within the community and the surrounding areas.

After 20 years, God anointed Deborah to be a prophet with the message of deliverance and victory. This was not supposed to be her swan song, but Barak refused to obey the prophecy unless the prophetess Deborah stood by his side in the deliverance of Israel (4:8). It was not uncommon to ask a prophet to go to battle with the military leader. Some interpreters see Barak's insistence only to have her bless the military before battle, not participate in the battle (see Saul, Samuel, and Nathan).

Yet, Deborah's directions from God was to prophesy to Barak, not to accompany him in battle. After much pressure from Barak (and the Lord giving her another word) Deborah agreed to go. However, she informed him that he would not get the victory, but rather a woman (Jael) would receive the credit because of his initial reluctance to obey the word of prophecy from the Lord.

DEBORAH: WHAT WAS HER MESSAGE?

"She sent and summoned Barak, son of Abinoam from Kedesh in Naphtali, and said to him, 'The Lord, the God of Israel, commands you, Go take position at Mt. Tabor, bringing 10,000 from the tribe of Naphtali and the tribe of Zebulun. I will draw out Sisera, the general of Jabin's army to meet you by the Wadi Kishon with his chariots and his troops; and I will give him into your hand.'"

—Judges 4:6-7

Deborah's message was a message of military victory over the enemies of Israel. The Lord God gave a message to Deborah to give to Barak the general of Israel's make-shift army. Israel's oppression by King Jabin of Canaan was coming to an end after 20 years. However, the military commander believed that the anointing needed to defeat the enemy was on Deborah, not him. So in his mind the only way the battle would be successful was if Deborah accompanied him. His response to the prophecy showed a lack of faith in the spoken word of God. This lack of faith took the credit for the guaranteed victory away from Barak and gave it over to Jael, the woman who drove a tent peg through the temple of Jabin's general Sisera.

Deborah's message is twofold: have faith in God's power to deliver Israel once again from the hands of her enemies, and victory comes despite Israel's constant apostasy against God's rule as their king. The people Israel did not learn from the previous situations regarding the earlier judges. Deborah knew that the time had come to stir up Israel. She received this knowledge directly from God. Deborah knew it was her responsibility to inform Israel "what thus says the Lord." In this light she followed in the footsteps of the prophetic tradition.

The word is never the word of the prophet but always a direct message from the Lord forecasting an event that is about to occur. Not only is the event pronounced, but the outcome as well. It then becomes the prophet's responsibility – whether they agree with the word or not – to proclaim the message to the directed audience. In this case it was Barak and the tribes of Naphtali and Zebulun. Deborah's prophesy came true. General Sisera was defeated and the credit was given to a woman (Jael).

The final message of Deborah is emphasized in The Song of Deborah. It celebrates her achievements and is one of the oldest examples of Hebrew literature still in existence (12th century BCE). The Song of Deborah reveals the underlining ancient theology and attitudes around the concept and belief in a God of War.

Her message intentionally characterized God as a "War God." Israel's release from Egyptian slavery did not entail a war or military battle. God revealed himself as a deliverer through the control and manipulation of nature. Eventually, the angel of death forced the Pharaoh's hand.

Now under the oppression of a new threat, Deborah's message was meant to remind Israel about the unlimited power of her God. The Canaanites were the more established and richer culture in comparison to Israel's government of a tribal confederacy. Militarily Canaan was more technologically advanced and used that technology to maintain power over the region for 20 years!

The Israelites cried out to the Lord, as they had on other occasions when oppressed by an enemy. Deborah was chosen to give a message of hope. The God of Israel had not forsaken them. Their time of punishment was coming to an end. They will be restored to their proper place as God's chosen people. God's power will again rise up against those who threaten his people.

In addition to the message portraying God as a God of war, Deborah's Song coincides with the themes of joy, thanksgiving, and praise. The narrative chose to use poetry to celebrate the military victory, similar to Miriam and the Song of Moses. The army expressed joy and thanksgiving for a victory that technically was not supposed to happen! Jabin's military had 900 iron chariots! So Deborah offered praise by encouraging her audience to "bless the Lord." Why? Because she compared the power of God and the weakness of Israel to the Canaanite human might. King Jabin and Sisera were no match for the power of an Almighty God.

There was no need to fear human might. Although all 12 tribes did not rally to the call to go to war, Deborah assured those 10,000 from the tribes of Naphtali and Zebulun that God was with them. God will fight their battle and give them the victory, just like he did with Moses and Joshua.

Deborah sang about how Sisera's mother waited in vain for her son's victorious return as he had done so many times before. But God used Jael, the wife of Heber the Kenite to bring down the threat of the mighty Sisera and the Canaanite army. Jael and Deborah allowed Israel to have rest for the next 40 years!

Judges 4 gives a prose narrative giving a more historical description of the event. But the poetry of Judges 5 heightens the contrast, giving way to language that is more creative, imaginary, and symbolic.

Chapter Three

HULDAH
WHO WAS SHE?

Wife, teacher, cousin to the prophet Jeremiah, prophetess

HULDAH: WHAT IS HER STORY?

The book of 2 Kings is the last of the historical books composed by the Deuteronomic Historian (DtH). The book of Kings was originally one long scroll, but when it was translated into the Greek (*the Septuagint*), which was a wordier version, the scrolls were divided into two separate scrolls. We find the names of the kings of both the northern kingdom Israel and the southern kingdom Judah. The histories run parallel. The DtH favored the southern kingdom and believed Judah was the proper legacy of King David.

In 2 Kings 22, we learn of a prophetess named Huldah. What brought Huldah into the limelight was the occasion in which King Josiah sought out her services as a prophetess. A lost Sefer Torah was found hidden in the walls of the renovated temple. In order to verify and validate its authenticity, King Josiah sent the High Priest Hilkiah, along with a delegation, to seek out Huldah's opinion on the status of the Sefer Torah.

There were several famed prophets active during this time period: Jeremiah, Zephaniah, Habakkuk, and Nahum.[42] Yet it was the prophetess Huldah that was sought out. Scholars disagree on why Huldah was chosen. Some say it was because Jeremiah was out of town[43]; others say it was because the King wanted a more compassionate prophecy from a woman's perspective.

---

[42] Miller, John W. *Meet the Prophets: A Beginners' Guide to the Books of the Biblical Prophets.* Paulist Press: New York, 1987, pp 139

[43] Jeremiah was out of town because God sent him to visit the Jewish exiles in Assyria where they had lived in captivity since the reign of Shalmaneser, King of Assyria. He conquered the northern 10 tribes. Jeremiah went there to bring them a message of encouragement and hope. God had not forgotten them and would soon gather them all and bring them back to Israel. Mindel, Nissan. *Huldah the Prophetess.* http://www.chabad.org/library/article_cdo/aid/112503/jewish/Huldah-the-Prophetess.htm. Pp 1-4

Whatever the reason, it was the authentication of Huldah, along with her prophecy, that determined the fate of Jerusalem and King Josiah.

So then, who is Huldah? We know from the scriptures (2 Kings 22:12-26) that she was married to Shallum, "Keeper of the wardrobe." This seems to imply that Shallum was responsible for the King's clothing. She is referred to in the scriptures as a prophetess, the only female prophet mentioned in the book of Kings.

Her family ties reveal that she is a kindred of Jeremiah. They were both descendants from Joshua and Rahab.[44] Huldah means *"weasel"* in Hebrew. In some cultures the weasel is the quintessential feminine creature, sometimes revered as a midwife, but also feared as a witch.[45] Laura Gibbs quotes Aaron Rothkoff as saying that Huldah was ascribed the name "weasel" because she was arrogant towards King Josiah when she referred to him as "the man" and not as king.[46]

Huldah was a woman of great intellect and insight. She was highly respected because of her great love for God. She was well-known as a voice of God.[47] Huldah was a woman of tremendous self-esteem. She was filled with the Holy Spirit and could speak on God's behalf.[48]

Huldah lived in Jerusalem in the Second Quarter, a place near the Temple. Yet King Josiah did not send for her, but sent a delegation to her residence seeking authentication of the recently discovered Sefer Torah.[49] According to the Targum, Huldah had a school where she taught publically. Legend then linked Huldah's school to the "Huldah Gates" in Jerusalem. While Jeremiah admonished and preached repentance to the men, she did likewise to the women.[50]

In the Aggadah, Huldah was one of 7 prophetesses mentioned by name

---

[44] Sperling, S. David and Fryma, Tiksia S. *The Jewish Virtual Library.* p 1
[45] Gibbs, Laura. *Myth-Folklore Course Diary.* http://religionsreading.blogspot.com/2007/06/bible-woman-huldah.html, p 2
[46] *Ibid.*
[47] Kimbrough, Marjorie. L. *She Is Worthy…* p 68
[48] *Ibid.,* p 67
[49] *Ibid.,* p 68
[50] Gibbs, Laura. *Myth-Folklore Course Diary.* p 2

in the bible.[51] In the Midrash 1:3, the "Gate of Huldah" in the temple was formerly the gate leading to Huldah's schoolhouse.[52] Huldah was not moved by the titles of men or intimated by their power and authority.[53] In the Megilla 14B it is argued that King Josiah sent delegates to the prophetess Huldah, as opposed to a male prophet because women prophets are more compassionate and that was the quality King Josiah sought from Huldah after hearing the severe punishment for not adhering to God's word.[54]

Huldah's tone contained a feminine tone of nurturing, sensitivity, and compassion according to the Talmudic citation. She gives King Josiah the encouragement and hope he needs in order to eradicate idolatry from the temple that was promoted by his late father, Amon.[55]

Yet, despite her limited biography in the scriptures, Huldah was a prophetess, a woman of great faith and moral character and possessed broad knowledge of the Torah. This combination of positive characteristics elevated Huldah to the level and position of a prophetess. Her identity is one that the authors of the Book of 2 Kings could not ignore.

---

[51] Sterling, S. David and Fryman, Tiksia S. *Jewish Virtual Library.* p 1

[52] *Ibid.*

[53] *Women Prophets in the Bible.* http://stronginfaith.org/article.php? p 90

[54] Neiman, Rachel. *Women in Judaism, the prophetess Huldah: her Message of Hope.* http://www.Torah.org/learning/women/class51.html. p 2

[55] *Ibid*, p 2

HULDAH: WHAT WAS HER MESSAGE?

"She declared to them, 'Thus says the Lord, the God of Israel: Tell the man who sent you to me, Thus says the Lord, I will indeed bring disaster on this place and on its inhabitants – all the words of the book that the king of Judah has read.'"

—2 Kings 22:15-16

Huldah did not go to the king to prophesy. The king sent a delegation, led by the High Priest, to her home for authentication of a Sefer Torah found in the temple wall during restoration. The reading of the Sefer Torah was so disturbing to King Josiah that he ripped his clothing. The Sefer Torah revealed how far away from God's laws Israel had moved during the rule of his father.

But before he could respond and act on a large scale to bring Israel back in line with God's holy word, King Josiah needed to make sure this book was authentic. This is where the prophetess Huldah comes into play. King Josiah recognized that in the midst of all the neglect of God's word, Huldah the prophetess, like her relative Jeremiah, remained faithful and was a true spokesperson for the Lord.[56]

Scott McKnight states the following in the face of some scholars trying to minimize Huldah's role in establishing the authenticity of the Sefer Torah, "Huldah is not chosen because no men were available; she is chosen because she is truly exceptional among the prophets."[57] Once Huldah read the Sefer Torah her message was two-fold: one of judgment for all of Israel; and one of peace for King Josiah.

THE JUDGMENT

When the Sefer Torah was brought to Huldah she knew immediately, under the unction of the Holy Spirit, that it was authentic. She said without hesitation, "Thus says the Lord, the God of Israel…" (2 Kgs 22:15). Huldah repeatedly used the phrase, "thus says the Lord," which was a familiar phrase of the Old Testament prophets announcing to the audience that it was the Lord and not Huldah speaking on her behalf.

Huldah verified the predictions of doom and gloom, as did the prophets before her. This judgment was the result of Israel's constant apostasy against the Lord God of Israel. Israel did not learn from the example of the Northern Kingdom destroyed in 721-22 B.C.E. by the Assyrians for the same abominations. Instead, corrupt kings and priests were allowed to rule Israel

---

[56] Horton. Stanley. *Rediscovering the Prophetic Role of Women.* http://enrichmentjournal.ag.org/2001-02/080_prophetic_role.cfm p 1

[57] *Ibid.* p 2

with greed and lustful appetites. They brought idol gods into God's holy temple to appease their foreign wives' religious devotions to the idol gods of their culture.

Huldah prophesied ultimate judgment. Her prophecy moved King Josiah to declare a religious revival take place immediately! This allowed Huldah to play an important part in the great spiritual revival that followed her prophecy.[58] However, the religious leaders did not heed her prophetic warning. Huldah was clear what the judgment entailed:

> *Thus says the Lord, the God of Israel: Tell the man who sent you to me, Thus says the Lord, I will indeed bring disaster in this place and on its inhabitants – all the words of the book that the king of Judah has read. Because they have abandoned me and have made offerings to other gods, so that they have provoked me to anger with all the work of their hands, therefore, my wrath will be kindled against this place, and it will not be quenched…. 2 Kgs 22:15-17-NRSV.*

It is believed by most scholars that this judgment is the response to the words of Deut 28:15-20:

> *The Lord will send upon you disaster, panic, and frustration in everything you attempt to do until you are destroyed and perish quickly, on account of the evil of your deeds, because you have forsaken me.*

This judgment is about to come to past unless King Josiah can turn things around and bring the people back to God as did the Judges. Jeremiah prophesied earlier but the religious leaders rejected him, beat him, and threw him in a pit because of his messages of prophecy from the Lord. Now Jeremiah has temporarily retreated in hopes that King Josiah's religious revival would make an impact on the religious leaders and change their hearts.

If King Josiah is successful God's wrath may be averted. However, according

---

[58] Mindel, Nissan. *Huldah the Prophetess.* http://www.chabad.org/library/article_cdo/aid/112503/jewish/Hulday-the-prophetess.htm. p 2

to the prophecy of Huldah, the punishment was irreversible. God was fed up with Israel's fickleness. Huldah's prophecy was fulfilled 35 years later.[59]

THE PROPHECY OF PEACE

Although the first part of Huldah's prophecy was total judgment upon Israel, the second part was a message of peace for the king himself:

> But as to the king of Judah, who sent you to inquire of the Lord, thus shall you say to him, 'Thus says the Lord, the God of Israel: Regarding the words that you have heard, because your heart was penitent, and you humbled yourself before the Lord, when you heard how I spoke against this place, and against its inhabitants, that they should become a desolation and a curse, and because you have torn your clothes and wept before me, I also have heard you, says the Lord. Therefore, I will gather you to your ancestors, and you shall be gathered to your grave in peace; your eyes shall not see all the disaster that I will bring on this place. -- 2 Kgs 22:18-20

Huldah prophesied that King Josiah would not live to witness the predicted judgment against Israel. Her message was that "the Lord will gather you to your ancestors, and you shall be gathered to your grave in peace." Biblical history records the death of King Josiah as violent, in the midst of battle against the Egyptians. These are not the words of Huldah's prophecy. What happened?

The book of Deuteronomy does not normally record a failed prophecy. As a matter of fact, the difference between a false prophet and a true prophet was whether or not their prophecy became a reality. So why did the second part of Huldah's prophecy fail?

Choon-Leong Seow argues that in light of the violent and horrible judgment that was pronounced on all the inhabitants of Judah, King Josiah's death leading his people in battle against an enemy, was peaceful. The king was

---

[59] Horton, Stanley. *Rediscovering the Prophetic Role of Women.* p 6

required to go to battle with his army. This gave the king honor and adoration of his people.[60]

The author of Deuteronomy states that all prophecy should be tested and if they do not come to pass, they should be ignored (Dt 18:20-22; Jere 28:9). However, some prophecies are contingent upon the recipient's response (see Jonah).[61] Why then did King Josiah die a violent death? Again the following argument attempts to address this seemingly false prophesy:

> Most prophecies of judgment are contingent upon our response. King Josiah died in battle because he blatantly ignored the command of God not to go to war against Meco, King of Egypt (2 Chron 35:22). If King Josiah had obeyed God and not leaned on his own understanding, then he would have surely died in peace.[62]

These are two different explanations for why Huldah's prophecy of peace regarding King Josiah's fate was not in sync with the word of the Lord. Huldah was compelled to report God's message word for word. The recipient, however, can either be obedient or disobedient thereby altering the prophetic outcome. It does not in any way invalidate the prophecy.

King Josiah lived another 13 years after Huldah's prophecy. He reigned a total of 31 years and did not live to witness the destruction of Jerusalem by the Babylonians in 586/87 B.C.E.

---

[60] Seow, Choon-Leong. *2 Kings 22:12-20: A Prophetic Oracle.* New Interpreter's Bible Commentary, vol 3: Abingdon Press: Nashville, 1999. p 278-82.
[61] *Women Prophets of the Bible.* p 90
[62] *Ibid.,* p 5

Chapter Four

ANNA
WHO WAS SHE?

Daughter, widow, teacher, prophetess

ANNA: WHAT IS HER STORY?

*A*nna is found in the Gospel of St. Luke. The Gospels were written accounts of the life, ministry and death of Jesus the Christ. Luke is the third gospel writer in the order of the New Testament. He was a physician by trade and was converted to Christianity under the tutelage of Paul the Apostle. Eventually, he became Paul's secretary and traveled with Paul throughout his missionary journeys. Luke is very "female friendly" and oftentimes acknowledges women in his accounts of Jesus and Paul's ministries.

Anna was the daughter of Phanuel. She was a member of the tribe of Asher. She was married for seven years before her husband died. Her husband's name is not given, which is unusual. Usually it is the woman who remains unnamed. The scriptures suggest that she was widowed for 84 years and married for only 7 years. That would put her at the ripe old age of 105 years old.

Luke tells us that she was a devout Jew who regularly practiced the discipline of fasting and prayer. The scripture tells us that she never left the temple, but remained there, day and night. This implied that she had residence in one of the temple rooms. That she was allowed to occupy one of the temple apartments spoke volumes about her character.[63] Let us look closer at the details about Anna's identity.

First of all, she was a prophetess. Anna means *"grace or favor"*. As a prophetess Anna foretold the future specifically in regards to the Christ. This role became prominent in her life after she was presented the baby Jesus in the temple. Secondly, Anna was a daughter. Her father was Phanuel. His

---

[63] Walsh. Sheila. *Anna the Prophetess: A Beautiful Life*. http://www.faithgateway.com/anna-prophetess-beautiful-life/#.U7HXQIVf4Ug. p 1

name means *"the face of God."* Anna and her father's name together means *"for grace proceeds from the face and mouth of God and is breathed into the faithful."* Her father's name is similar to the place where Jacob met God face to face in Gen 32:30 (Peniel).

Thirdly, Anna was from the tribe of Asher. Asher is one of the 10 tribes who originally inhabited the western portion of the region of Galilee. According to the book of Genesis, the tribe of Asher was one of the tribes of Israel. Jacob blessed his son Asher stating that "Asher's food shall be rich, and he shall provide royal delicacies" (Gen 49:20). Moses blessed Asher in this way, "Most blessed of sons be Asher; may he be the favorite of his brothers, and may he dip his foot in oil. Your bars are iron and bronze; and as your days, so is your strength" (Dt 33:24).

The book of Joshua records the successful conquest of Canaan. Joshua allocated the land among the 12 tribes. The tribe of Asher received its territory after Joshua cast lots for the unconquered land. Once the land was conquered it was divided between 7 of the 12 tribes who had not yet received their allotment. The fifth lot fell on Asher (Josh 19:24-31).

The tribe was named after the younger of two sons born to Jacob and Zilpah, the maidservant of Leah. Leah was Jacob's first wife that he did not love because her father tricked him on his wedding night. Jacob worked 7 years for his first love, Rachel, but because she was the youngest, Leah had to be wed first. So in the dark of night, and full of wine, he inadvertently slept with Leah on his wedding night. The name means "happy" because Leah said, "Happy am I, for the daughters will call me blessed and she called him Asher" (Gen 30:13).

The families and sons of Asher were numbered 53,400 when they entered the Promised Land (Nu 26: 44-47; I Chronicles 7:30-40). According to historians and archaeologists Asher became identified with the great Phoenician Empire and the cities of Tyre and Sidon. Today the modern tribe of Asher is found in S. Africa, Belgium and Luxemburg.

This was Anna's heritage. John Macarthur says this in regards to Anna's lineage:

Anna's descent from the tribe of Asher suggests that her heritage owed much to God's grace. Her ancestors had either migrated south before the Assyrian conquest of Israel, or they were among the small and scattered groups of exiles who returned from captivity. Anna was a part of a believing remnant from the northern kingdom, and she was therefore, a living emblem of God's faithfulness to His people."[64]

Fourthly Anna was a widow. Luke tells us that Anna was married for 7 years (2:37). If she was married by age 15, which was common practice, then she would have been 22 when her husband died, still very young and could have remarried. Yet, she gave herself to the service of God. This was not unusual in the New Testament period. Her role would be similar to a Nun in the Catholic Church today.

Widowhood was extremely difficult, especially if you had no sons to support you. You were most likely sentenced to a life of poverty. This is why Paul urged young widows to remarry (I Cor 7:9). A widow without sons or a male heir to support her, had to depend on the kindness of strangers or as a servant to other family members. [65] Her life was not extravagant, but fugal. She was chaste and sober. Prostitution was an option for some, but frowned upon by the religious community.

Instead, Anna chose a life of prayer and fasting, night and day. She lived on the temple's grounds from whence she spread her message to other women who may have experienced her plight as a widow. According to Nehemiah 13:7-9, there were apartments in the outer court of the temple. These were modest chambers used by priests who lived on the temple grounds. The priests were required to give at least 2 weeks of service in the temple.[66]

Anna was no longer at the age to serve as a possible caretaker of the temple. Therefore, because of her long years of faithfulness, she may have been given a small room to reside in now that she was almost 100 years old.

---

[64] Macarthur, John. *Twelve Extraordinary Women.* Nelson Books: Nashville, 2005, p 135

[65] *Ibid.,* p 136

[66] *Ibid.,* p 137

She was always in the temple so allowing her a space to minister to other women was a blessing for her and the temple personnel.[67]

The Catholic and Orthodox churches consider Anna as a saint. The Orthodox Church in particular consider Anna and Simeon the *"God-Receivers"* and the last prophets of the Old Testament. They are observed on Feb 3 and 16, as the Synaxis (after feast) following the Presentation of the Christ Child.[68]

Icons of Anna exist in the Presentation of Christ to her by his parents Mary and Joseph. In the depiction of Anna, she is behind Mary with her hands raised to show people Him as Christ, or hands a scroll which is attributed often to prophets in Orthodox iconography.[69] "The Orthodox Church tradition considers that Christ met his people, Israel, in the persons of Simeon and Anna."[70]

---

[67] *Ibid.*

[68] *Anna the Prophetess.* http://en.wikipedia.org/wiki/Anna_the_Prophetess, p 2

[69] *Ibid.*

[70] *Strong in the Faith.* http://stronginfaith.org/article.php?p=90, p 2

WHAT WAS ANNA'S MESSAGE?

*She never left the temple but worshiped there
with fasting and prayer night and day.
At that moment she came, and began to praise
God and to speak about the child to all who
were looking for the redemption of Jerusalem*

—Luke 2:37b-38

The word *"prophetess"* simply designates a woman who spoke the word of God. She is uniquely devoted to proclaiming what *"Thus says the Lord!"* when she receives a message from God. Some say Anna was called a prophetess because it was her habit to declare the truth of God's word to others.[71] Anna's hopes and dreams were full of messianic expectation. She was blessed by God to be one of a few key witnesses who knew and understood the significance of Jesus' entrance into history.

It was the revelation declared by Simeon and Anna in an encounter with the baby Jesus that caused her to prophesy a new message from God. No longer was the message about expectation and anticipation of the Promised Messiah's arrival. Now her message was that He is here – Emmanuel! Simeon had long awaited to see the Promised Messiah. He prayed to God to allow his eyes to see the salvation of his people through the work of the Promised Messiah of the Old Testament, before he died.

When Simeon confirmed the baby Jesus as God's answer to his prayers, the prophetess Anna overheard the prophetic declaration. She too awaited this good news. Now, along with Simeon, her fasting and prayer life was reaping the benefits of seeing with her own eyes the Messiah. Anna was now a living witness! Her new message will encompass her new revelation.

What was Anna's New Message?

Anna's many years of petition to God turned to praise that day in the temple.[72]

> Anna was one of a godly remnant in Israel who looked for the DaySpring from on high. As she heard Simeon's praise for prophecy fulfilled, she went out to her godly intimates to declare the glad tidings. Faith through her long years of waiting

---

[71] Macarthur, John. *12 Extraordinary Women...* p 133
[72] *"Anna: The First Woman who became the First Christian Missionary."* http://www.biblegateway.com/devotionals/all-women-bible/2011/07/26 Zondervan, 1988

was rewarded and she became the first female herald of the incarnation to all who look for the Redeemer in Jerusalem.[73]

Anna's prophetic message was 2-fold: the past is now fulfilled and the salvation of Israel is at hand. Both messages are connected to the birth of Jesus the Christ Child.

THE PAST IS NOW FULFILLED

According to John Macarthur, the messianic expectation was running at an all-time high in the early first century.[74] Prophecies found in the Old Testament book of Daniel announced the period of 483 years would past before the Messianic Prince would be born. Macarthur continues to connect the decree of Artaxerxes (445 BCE) (Ne 2:1-8) with the lunar calendar of 360 days. From this calculation the Messiah Prince would appear around the year 30 CE, which was the year of Jesus' triumphant entry.[75]

Many thought John the Baptist was the Messiah Prince (Lk 3:15; Jn 1:27-37) but John quickly put that rumor to rest acknowledging that he was not worthy to untie the Messiah Prince's sandals (Lk 3:16). The first century was anxiously waiting for someone who would fit the bill. They were looking in the wrong places and when Jesus came, they did not recognize him as the Messiah Prince. Jesus' birth was lowly, and with the exception of the Wise Men from Mesopotamia, those who recognized and accepted Jesus were of lowly backgrounds –the shepherds, Mary and Joseph, Simeon and Anna.

The final witness of the birth of the Messiah Prince is the prophetess Anna. We know who she is – of lowly stature (female and a widow with no sons). Yet she was chosen by God to acknowledge and proclaim that a long period of prophecy had come to an end.

She lived in the temple and was at the right place at the right time. Appearing at Simeon's side, she witnessed and overheard Simeon's proclamation regarding the identity of the Christ Child. Simeon and Anna were the last of

---

[73] *Ibid.*

[74] Macarthur, John. *12 Extraordinary Women…* p 129

[75] *Ibid.* p 129-30

the prophetic tradition. Their hopes and dreams were fulfilled the moment Mary and Joseph came into the temple to have the Messiah Prince blessed.

Simeon's prophecy about the destiny and effect of Jesus' ministry and that God had empowered his prayer to see the Lord's Messiah before he died impacted Anna's message of completion and she saw the beginnings of a new religious era that would bring Israel into a new path of salvation. The future blessing of Israel now laid in the hands of a baby boy.[76]

A NEW DOOR TO GOD'S SALVATION

Anna's second message is her response to what she overheard in Simeon's prophecy.

> *At that moment she came, and began to praise God and to speak about the child to all who were looking for the redemption of Jerusalem (Lk 2:38)*

As a response to being a witness to the Christchild, Anna immediately began to prophesy and spread the good news to all. Her audience is described as "all who were looking for the redemption of Jerusalem." What this says is that not all were waiting for the fulfillment of the Messiah prophecy. The religious leaders had become so hard-hearted and self-absorbed that they no longer "watched as well as prayed" for the arrival of the Messiah. They were satisfied with things as they were, which was to their advantage and supported their greed.

While the poor in the land suffered spiritually, physically, emotionally, and financially, the Romans, the Sadducees, the Pharisees, and the tax collectors, all profited at their expense and from their pain and oppression. Hope that the coming Messiah's prophecy would come true in their lifetime was fading. Those that held on to the hope believed that the Messiah would deliver them from their oppressive situation and restore Israel to its days of glory. Rome will be annihilated and all the enemies of God will be run out of the Promised

---

[76] *Biblegate.com*

Land. This belief was especially held by the political group known as the Zealots.

So Anna's message was long overdue and gave new hope to some and a renewed hope to others. This message was directly connected to Simeon's prophecy in Luke 2:29-32:

> *Master, now you are dismissing your servant in peace, according to your word; for my eyes have seen your salvation, which you have prepared in the presence of all peoples, a light for revelation to the Gentiles and for glory to your people Israel. (NRSV)*

Anna could not contain her excitement after she heard Simeon's prophecy. Her message to all who received it was that Jesus the Messiah Prince, spoken about in the book of Daniel, was not only returning God's glory to Israel, but now has opened the door to salvation to the Gentiles as well! The Christ Child has come to be a light of revelation to the Gentiles as well as to Israel.

The Jews were expecting a new door for salvation to be opened with the coming of the Christ Child, but that was not the end of it as prophesied by the minor prophet Second Isaiah (Isa 40-55). In the prophecy of Second Isaiah, now Gentiles from other nations are included:

> *See, I made him a witness to the peoples, a leader and commander for the peoples. See, you shall call nations that you do not know, and nations that do not know you shall run to you because of the Lord your God, the Holy One of Israel, for he has glorified you (Isa 55:44).*

Although Anna appears in only a few verses in Luke 2, her life and testimony showed her commitment and loyalty to God. She understood the significance of Jesus' birth. She made no attempt to keep it to herself. Therefore, she became one of the first and most enduring witnesses to Christ. Everything she had been praying and fasting for was suddenly right in front of her. She knew, like Simeon, that God had answered her prayers. This revelation and acknowledgment fueled her message to proclaim to her audience and the people of Jerusalem that the day of the Lord had finally come. That message served as a bridge from the past prophecies about the Promised Messiah to His actual arrival. She spent many years talking to God; and became known best for talking to people about the Christ. This became her message for the rest of her life.[77]

Anna was a prophetess whose heart was prepared for the coming Messiah. She was known to declare the truth of God's word to others – the Jews and now the Gentiles. She had a reputation as a gifted teacher for other women and a faithful encourager of her fellow worshippers in the temple.[78] Abraham Kuyper sums it up in these words:

> Thus it was whispered about in the Temple that the hour of redemption was at hand, that the fullness of time had come, and that the Saviour of the world should arise out of that holy child. When Anna had confirmed that, her task had been fulfilled. Her testimony in the Temple was the last voice of prophecy heard. Prophecy had served its purpose. John, the Herald of the Lord, was standing at the gates.[79]

---

[77] Macarthur, John. *12 Extraordinary Women*… p139
[78] *Ibid.* p 132-33
[79] Kuyper, Abraham. *Women of the New Testament*. Grand Rapids MI: Zondervan Publishing House, p 21

Chapter Five

THE DAUGHTERS OF PHILIP
WHO WERE THEY?

Daughters, siblings, virgins, prophetesses

THE DAUGHTERS OF PHILIP: WHAT IS THEIR STORY?

*T*he book of Acts is the second volume of Luke's Gospel. It is the historical account of the birth and growth of the Christian church. Its official name is *The Acts of the Apostles* but it does not mention or highlight the work of many of them. The first half of the book focuses on Peter and the Pentecost experience. The second half focuses on Paul and his missionary journeys.

Our earliest evidence of the church is the letters of Paul. The church by then had been in existence for at least twenty years. When we examine the authentic letters of Paul (*I Thessalonians, Galatians, Philippians, I and 2 Corinthians, Philemon and Romans*) we get a clear picture of the participation, power, and leadership by women within the communities of faith.[80]

Women were included as full members of the Christian communities. Luke's Gospel contains evidence that social context of the day was influenced by the Christian message. Luke provides the written evidence about women and their ministry with Jesus.[81]

We first hear about the four daughters of Philip in Luke's account in Acts 21:8-9:

> *The next day we left and came to Caesarea; and we went into the house of Philip the evangelist, one of seven, and stayed with him. He had four unmarried daughters who had the gift of prophecy (NRSV)*

---

[80] Scroggs, Robin. *Women and Men in the Early Church*. We Belong Together: Churches in Solidarity with Women. Cunningham, Sarah ed. New York: Friendship Press, pp 44-45

[81] MacHaffie, Barbara J. *Her Story: Women in Christian Tradition*. Philadelphia: Fortress Press, p 24

The biblical account of Philip's four daughters is found only here. We know more about their father Philip and the role he played in the functioning of the disciples after Jesus' ascension. There is much debate about whether or not Philip is one of the original apostles or one of the seven appointed by the apostles to do the everyday mundane (though important) task of feeding the Greek widows (Acts 6:5).

The debate over Philip's true identity is the result of differing historical accounts made first by Papias (60-130 CE) and Polycrates (130-196 CE). Later Eusebius, a historian and a theologian of the latter half of the first century, uses his predecessors as resources for his account of the identity of Philip.[82] Eusebius assumed the earlier reports were accurate.

However, the person and message of the 4 daughters is not directly affected by who their father was. The religious climate of the day was energized and supported the events of the crucifixion and resurrection. Eventually tradition has Philip as the bishop of Tralles.[83]

The Greek word used in Acts 21:9 for prophecy is *"propheteuo"* which means *"to prophesy, to be a prophet, speak forth by divine inspirations, to predict."*[84] Based on the use of the word prophecy in this instance, the 4 daughters were prophets.

The scripture is unclear on how often these 4 women prophesied but that is also the case with male prophets. We read of male prophesies frequently in the Old Testament, yet the frequency of their prophecies do not verify nor negate their legitimacy as prophets. In the Old Testament the one criteria for determining the authenticity of a true prophet was whether or not their prophecies came true. Oftentimes it was their disciples who revisited their master's prophecies after they were deceased.

Acts 21:7 reports that Paul was on his third missionary journey when he entered the house of Philip. He and his traveling companions had just left Tyre and arrived at Plotemais. The next day they arrived in Caesaria and as

---

[82] *Eusebius History Eccl 3:31.3* Interpreter's Dictionary of the Bible. vol 3. Abingdon: Nashville, 1962. p 311

[83] *Ibid.*, p 785

[84] *Strong In the Faith; Women Prophets in the Bible.* p 6

was customary, resided in the house of a fellow believer. This believer was Philip and his four daughters.

Paul seemed not to challenge or question the four daughters' status as prophetesses. Paul felt the gift of prophesy ranked high on his list of spiritual gifts (I Cor 14:3). Prophets played an important role in the early church.

The fact that these 4 ladies are cited by high level historical and theological sources suggests that the daughters of Philip were popular, credible, and committed to the gospel message. They were held in high regard as prophetesses according to Papias.[85] Eusebius referred to them as "great lights" or "mighty luminaries."[86] Those who came against the behavior of the prophetesses of Montanism referred to the 4 daughters of Philip as role models for their demeanor and discipline in religious settings.[87]

The 4 daughters were of the age of accountability and were Jewish Christian women who lived with their father in his home in Caesarea in Judea. They possessed the gift of prophecy and are literally called "virgins" (partheus) – prophesizing daughters. The fact that they were called "virgins" tells us that they were concerned about the things of the Lord, holy in body and in spirit, and undistracted.[88]

These 4 women were evidence of the prophecy of Joel that was restated at Pentecost by Peter (Joel 2:28-29). In the early church women were gifted with prophecy (I Cor 11:5; Rev 2:20). They were able to continue in the legacy of female prophets of the Old Testament such as Miriam, Deborah, the wife of Isaiah, Huldah and others. Some scholars believe that Luke had no choice but to mention Philip's daughters because of their prominence in the community.[89] Others argue that Luke was a promoter of women and included women in

[85] Riss, Rev. Kathryn J. *Women in Church History – Women Prophets.* http://godswordtowomen.org/prophets.htm, p 3

[86] Mowczko, Margaret. *Philip's Prophesying Daughters.* http://newlife.id.au/equality-and-gender-issues/philips-prophesying-daughters/ Nov 24, 2013. p 5

[87] *Ibid.,* p 3

[88] Plampin, Carolyn Goodman. *The Four Daughters of Philip Who Were Preachers.* Series Lessons on Christian Women. May 24, 2005. http://www.theotrek.org/resources/Plampin/Lessons-on-Christian-Women/4daughters.htm p 7

[89] O'Day, Gail R. *The Women's Bible Commentary, Acts.* Newsome, Carol A. and Ringer, Sharon H., eds. Louisville: Westminster John Knox, 1992, p 7

the establishment of the early church.[90] However, each daughter was unique in her own way, with gifts from God.[91] Although unique in their own way, they all chose to dedicate themselves to the service of God. They all spoke on God's behalf.[92]

Why were these 4 women so committed to God's service? Speculation starts with Philip's name. In the Greek his name comes from the verb *"pileo"* which means "I love." However, his daughters are nameless, although some historians have tried to investigate this unknown and came up with two of the 4 daughters' names: Hermione and Eutychis – from the Greek Menaon, an annual calendar which preserves the memories of martyrs and saints.[93]

Perhaps Philip's name was an expression of his character and personality. As an evangelist and one of the 7 chosen because he was spirit filled, Philip's obvious love for God was shared with families and believers. Their household must have been filled with the love of God and these 4 women were so moved by the example shown by their parents, that perhaps they too became convicted and committed. This eventually led to their call to prophesy and they allowed God to use them to encourage others in this ministry. Philip made the gospel real in his everyday life and his 4 daughters were challenged when God's word consumed them and gifted them with the word of prophecy.[94]

The Acts account tells us three things about the 4 daughters of Philip: 1) they were nameless; 2) they were virgins; 3) they prophesied. It is easy to elaborate and speculate more about these daughters of Philip. Many historians and theologians have done so over the centuries. The Roman Catholic Church has named them the first nuns.[95]

It is said that Eutychis was buried in Ephesus and Hermione may have been martyred. Other accounts claim that Philip along with his daughters,

[90] Massey, Lesly F. *"Women and the New Testament: An Analysis of Scripture in Light of New Testament Era Culture.* Jefferson City: McFarland & Co, 1989, p 81

[91] Mitchell, Ella Pearson, ed. *To Preach or not to Preach.* Valley Forge: Judson Press, 1991, p 101

[92] *Ibid.*

[93] Mowczko, Margaret. *Philip's Prophesying Daughters,* p 3

[94] Mitchell, Ella Pearson. *To Preach or Not to Preach,* p 103

[95] *The Daughters of Philip. Acts 21:8.* All the Women of the Bible. https://www.biblegateway.com/resources/all-women-bible/Daughters-Philip, p 3

are all buried in Caesarea.[96] It has also been reported by Eusebius that one of the 4 daughters died and was brought back to life.[97] The prophetic activity of these 4 women was so admired that a thousand years after Eusebius, a man named Nicephorus Callistus Xanthapoulas wrote a history about the church and mentioned the 4 daughters of Philip. He says the following about the 4 daughters of Philip:

> And until the time of Trajon these (successors of the Apostles) continued the priesthood, while the beloved disciple still was present in this life (John)… After them Quadralus became eminent in the prophetic gifts, being distinguished together with the daughters of Philip…[98]

Some people think that only men can be prophets. But the Bible mentions many women who served as prophets and some who were even called prophets. Although it may seem that prophecy had all but ceased by the time of the birth of Jesus, even in the time of little prophecy, there were women prophets. Women have served as prophets during all times. Sometimes they served alongside men in their own right (Huldah). Sometimes they were called especially because men were too weak in leadership (Deborah). There were even false women prophets (Noadiah/Neh 6:14; and Jezebel Rev 12).

In the book of Acts there are only ten words about the 4 daughters of Philip found in the New Testament. But they were considered great preachers and great lights by all who knew them and knew of them. Women served as prophets at the time of Jesus (Anna) and in the early church period. God has always anointed prophets both male and female, to deliver His word to His people and others who needed to heed to what "thus says the Lord."

---

[96] *Ibid.*

[97] Mowczko, Margaret. *Philip's Prophesying Daughters*, p 3

[98] *Ibid.*, p 4

WHAT WAS THEIR MESSAGE?

"The next day we left and came to Caesarea, and we went into the house of Philip the evangelist, one of the seven, and stayed with him. He had four unmarried daughters which had the gift of prophecy."

—*Acts 21:8-9*

Luke is unclear on what exactly or how frequently the 4 daughters of Philip prophesied. Prophesying in the New Testament era was meant to edify, exhort, and bring comfort to the Christians who encountered much oppression and persecution. (I Cor 14:3-4). Prophecy was given for learning and for comfort (I Cor 14:31). On occasion these women foretold of future events (I Pet 1:10). Their message may have been multiple in number according to the circumstances, situation, and audience.[99]

Some scholars believe their message was not singled out or recorded because it was the same message and theme as their male counterparts. The prophetic message was 3-fold: 1) God is loving; 2) God saves; 3) God wants justice for the poor.[100] The 4 daughters probably traveled with their father because of security and cultural reasons. While Philip tended to the male audience, his 4 daughters confined their ministry to the female believers.[101]

The purpose of the gift of prophecy was to confirm the word of God and to help those who heard the message know that it was from God. Therefore, the 4 daughters provided guidance, instruction, strengthening, encouragement, and comfort (Acts 13:3-4; 16:6; I Cor 14:3, 31).

Eusebius records that people traveled great distances to visit the daughters of Philip and listen to them as they taught the gospel message and retold stories about the events surrounding the early church and its ministry. They ministered along with the Apostle John and shared his stories about people being raised from the dead.[102] Eusebius also states that the 4 daughters, along with Quadratus, took over the ministry of the beloved disciple John when he passed away. John's community was based in the city of Ephesus.[103]

The message of the 4 daughters also focused on revealing to the early church God's plan for salvation and how they must live in order to please

---

[99] *Strong In the Faith.* p 6

[100] *Why Was there no Female Prophet in the Biblical History?* http://au.answers.yahoo.com/question/index?qid=20121015072301AA5zxWE p 1

[101] *Daughters of Philip.* All the Women of the Bible, p 3

[102] Mowczko, Margaret. *Philip's Prophesying Daughters,* p 3

[103] *Ibid.*

God.[104] There was no New Testament so it was necessary for those with the gift of prophecy to proclaim God's will to new converts.[105] The 4 daughters were bold in their proclamation of the gospel message. They were witnesses and worked signs and wonders as evidence of the anointing of the Holy Spirit. They preached and performed wonders among the people.

Luke described the works of those designated as prophets to exhort (*parakaleo*) and to strengthen (*episterize*) the disciples. This description is inclusive of both male and female prophets.[106]

In conclusion, it has been well documented by Church historians *(Eusebius)* and religious leaders *(Luke)* that the four daughters of Philip were special anointed women of God. They were given the gift of prophecy and because of their commitment to their calling and to God, these 4 ladies earned a place in biblical history (though only 10 written words) that cannot be denied or negated by those who wish to subordinate the role of women in the biblical period.

These women became role models and sources of inspiration for all women who believe the calling of God is on their lives. These women give courage to all to stand up and declare in the words of Isaiah 6, *"Here I am, send me."*

---

[104] Rushmore, Rebecca. *Philip's Daughters.* Gospel Gezette. http://www.gospelgazette.com/gazette/1999/jun/page13.shtml, p 3

[105] *Ibid.*

[106] *Ibid.,* p 4

Conclusion

The Old Testament scripture – Joel 2:28 (*Your sons and your daughters shall prophesy…*) and the New Testament scripture – Gal 3:28 (*In Christ there is no male or female…*) are two of the most famous scriptures that support the equality of women in the biblical period. The biblical authors did not avoid recording seemingly contradictions of cultural practices in regards to the treatment of women (Paul – I Cor 11). These two scriptures in particular have contributed to the hope for equality among all believers in the Church. It has not yet been achieved.

However, glimmers of hope for equality can be read throughout the bible. Examples of heroines and anointed women called by God to do God's bidding continue to reinforce the fact that God is no respecter of persons (*Ruth, Esther*). It is the heart that God judges, and the ability to be obedient that gets God's attention, not one's gender.

When the church chooses to accept whoever God calls without any prejudicial response, then perhaps once again, the Church can be a beacon of hope and salvation for "whosoever will" instead of a place of oppression, submission, and denial for those who are not male in gender or have color in their skin. Until then, the practice of racism, sexism and classism will continue to function as a "black eye" on the physical Church built by the One who declared, "Upon this rock I will build my Church and the gates of hell (*racism, sexism, classism*) shall not prevail against it."

Bibliography

GENERAL WORKS

Brueggeman, Walter. *Exodus*. New Interpreters Bible Commentary. V 1. Nashville: Abingdon, 1998

Buswell, Sara. *The Challenge of Old Testament Women 2*. Grand Rapids: Baker Book House, 1987

Cunningham, Sarah, ed. *We Belong Together: Churches in Solidarity with Women*. New York: Friendship Press, 1992

Fabella, Virginia, M.M. and Oduyoye, Mercy Amber. eds. *With Passion and Compassion: 3rd World Women Doing Theology*. 2nd edition. Maryknoll, NY: Orbis, 1989

Freedman, David Noel. Ed *The Interpreter's Dictionary of the Bible*. Nashville: Abingdon Press, 1962

Gonzalez, Justo L. *Acts: The Gospel of the Spirit*. New York: Orbis, 2001.

Harris, Stephen L. *Understanding the Bible*. 8th ed. New York: McGraw-Hill, 2011

Harvey, D. *"Hulday"*. Interpreter's Dictionary of the Bible, v 2. Nashville: Abingdon, 1962

Heine, Susanne. *Women in Early Christianity: A Reappraisal*. Minneapolis: Augsburg, Trans. John Bowden, 1988

Jensen, Mary E. *Bible Women Speak to Us Today*. Minneapolis: Augsburg, 1983

Jervell, Jacob. *"The Daughters of Abraham: Women in Acts."* The Unknown Paul: Essays on Luke-Acts and Early Christian History. Minneapolis: Augsburg, 1984

Kimbrough, Marjorie L. *She Is Worthy: Encounters with biblical Women*. Nashville: Abingdon Press, 1994

Kuyper, Abraham. *Women of the New Testament*. Grand Rapids: Zondervan, 1979

MacHaffie, Barbara J. *Her Story: Women in Christian Tradition*. Philadelphia: Fortress 1986.

Macarthur, John. *12 Extraordinary Women*. Nashville: Nelson Books, 2005

Massey, Lesly F. *"Women and the New Testament"*. Women and the New Testament: Analysis of Scripture in Light of New Testament Era Culture. Jefferson City: McFarland and Co, 1989

Mitchell, Ella Pearson. *Women: to Preach or Not to Preach*. Valley Forge: Judson Press, 1991.

O'Day, Gail R. *The Women's Bible Commentary, Acts*. Newsome, Carol A. and Ringer, Sharon H. eds. Louisville: Westminster John Knox Press, 1992

Olson, Dennis T. *"Deborah"*. New Interpreter's Bible Commentary, vol 2. Nashville: Abingdon Press, 1998

Reimer, Ivoni Richter. *Women in the Acts of the Apostles: A Feminist Liberation Perspective*. Minneapolis, Fortress, 1995

Reuther, Rosemary Radford, ed *Religion and Sexism: Images of Women in the Jewish and Christian Traditions.* New York: Simon and Schuster, 1974

Scanzoni, Letha D. and Hardesty, Nancy A. *All Were Meant To Be.* Nashville: Abingdon Press, 1986

Seim, Turid Karisen. *The Double Message: Patterns of Gender in Luke-Acts.* Nashville: Abingdon Press, 1994

Seow-Choon-Leong. *"A Prophetic Oracle".* New Interpreter's Bible Commentary, v 3 Nashville: Abingdon Press, 1998

Siddons, Philip. *Speaking Out For Women – A Biblical View.* Valley Forge: Judson Press, 1980

Vivione, Pauline A. *"Huldah"* Anchor Bible Dictionary. Freedman, David Noel, ed. v 3 New York: Doubleday, 1992

Watson, Elizabeth. *Daughters of Zion.* Richmond, Ind: Friends United Press, 1982

Williams, Michael E., ed. *The Storyteller's Companion to the Bible. Old Testament Women.* v 4. Nashville: Abingdon Press, 1993

WEBSITES

Gibbs, Laura. *"Myth-Folklore Course Diary".* http://religionsreading.blogspot.come/2007/06/bible-woman-huldah.html

Horton, Stanley. *Rediscovering the Prophetic Role of Women.* http://enrichmentjournal.ag.org/2001-02/080_prophetic_role.cfm, 2014

Kraft, Vicki. *"Miriam".* https://bible.org//seriespage/lesson-1-miriam. July 2007

Lockyer, Herbert. *"Anna"*. All the Women of the Bible. Bible Gateway Devotionals. http://www.biblegateway.com/devotionals/all-women-bible/2011/07/26. July 26, 2011

_____ *"Anna: The Woman who became the First Christian Missionary."* http://www.biblegateway.com/devotionals/all-women-bible. Zondervan, 1988

Mindel, Nissan. *"Miriam."* www.chabad.org/library/Miriam.htm

_____. *"Huldah the Prophetess."* http://www.chabad.org/library/article_cdo/aid/112503/jewish/Hulday-the-prophetess.htm

Mowczko, Margaret. *"Philip's Prophesying Daughters."* http://newlife.id.au/equality-and-gender-issues/philips-prophesying-saughters/nov24,2013

Neiman, Rachel. *Women in Judaism, the prophetess Huldah: her Message of Hope."* http://www.Torah.org/learning/women/class5/.html

Plampin, Carolyn Goodman. *"The Four Daughters of Philip Who Were Preachers."* Series Lessons on Christian Women. http://www.theotrek.org/resources/Plampin/Lessons-on-Christian-Women/4daughters.htm May 24, 2005

Riss, Rev. Kathryn J. *"Women in Church History-Women Prophets."* http://godswordtowomen.org/prophets.htm

Rothkoff, Aaron. *"Huldah: The Jewish Virtual Library."* Sperling, S. David and Fryma, Tiksia S. eds.www.jewishvirtuallibrary.org/huldah

Rushmore, Rebecca. *Philip's Daughters.* Gospel Gezette. http://www.gospelgazette.com/gazette/1999/jun/page13.shtml 2005

Walsh, Sheila. *"Anna the Prophetess: A Beautiful Life."* http://www.faithgateway.com/anna-prophetess-beautiful-life/#.U7HXQIVf4Ug. Sept 7, 2013

"Anna the Prophetess: http://en.wikipedia.org/wiki/Anna_the_Prophetess. June 28, 2014

"Female Prophets: Miriam, Deborah, Huldah, Noadiah, Anna." http://stronginfaitht. org/article.php?p=90, 2007

"The Feast of the Prophetess Anna." The New Movement. http:// newtheologicalmovement.blogspot.com/2011/09/feast-of-prophetess-anna-who-was-she.html

"The Daughters of Philip: Acts 21:8" All the Women of the Bible. http:// wwwbiblegateway.com/resources/all-women-bible/Daughers-Philip Zondervan, 1988

"Why Was There No Female Prophets in the Biblical History?" http://au.answers. yahoo.com/question/index?qid=20121015072301AA5zxWE

Printed in the United States
By Bookmasters